Cocker Spaniels

Cocker Spaniel Breeding, Diet, Rescue, Adoption, Temperament, Where to Buy, Cost, Health, Lifespan, Care Types, and Much More Included!

By Lolly Brown

Copyrights and Trademarks

All rights reserved. No part of this book may be reproduced or transformed in any form or by any means, graphic, electronic, or mechanical, including photocopying, recording, taping, or by any information storage retrieval system, without the written permission of the author.

This publication is Copyright ©2016. Nevada. All products, graphics, publications, software and services mentioned and recommended in this publication are protected by trademarks. In such instance, all trademarks & copyright belong to the respective owners. For information consult www.NRBpublishing.com

Disclaimer and Legal Notice

This product is not legal, medical, or accounting advice and should not be interpreted in that manner. You need to do your own due-diligence to determine if the content of this product is right for you. While every attempt has been made to verify the information shared in this publication, neither the author, neither publisher, nor the affiliates assume any responsibility for errors, omissions or contrary interpretation of the subject matter herein. Any perceived slights to any specific person(s) or organization(s) are purely unintentional.

We have no control over the nature, content and availability of the web sites listed in this book. The inclusion of any web site links does not necessarily imply a recommendation or endorse the views expressed within them. We take no responsibility for, and will not be liable for, the websites being temporarily unavailable or being removed from the internet.

The accuracy and completeness of information provided herein and opinions stated herein are not guaranteed or warranted to produce any particular results, and the advice and strategies, contained herein may not be suitable for every individual. Neither the author nor the publisher shall be liable for any loss incurred as a consequence of the use and application, directly or indirectly, of any information presented in this work. This publication is designed to provide information in regard to the subject matter covered.

Neither the author nor the publisher assume any responsibility for any errors or omissions, nor do they represent or warrant that the ideas, information, actions, plans, suggestions contained in this book is in all cases accurate. It is the reader's responsibility to find advice before putting anything written in this book into practice. The information in this book is not intended to serve as legal, medical, or accounting advice.

Foreword

The Cocker Spaniel is a name given to two separate breeds of dog – the American Cocker Spaniel and the English Cocker Spaniel. Cocker Spaniels were developed as hunting dogs but today they are commonly kept as companion pets. The Cocker Spaniel has a cheerful temperament and an affectionate nature – plus, these dogs are smart and very trainable. Cocker Spaniels are also a very attractive breed, having a long silky coat and soft, furry ears.

If you are considering the Cocker Spaniel breed for yourself or your family, do yourself a favor and learn as much as you can about these lovely dogs. The Cocker Spaniel is a wonderful breed but it is not the right choice for everyone. The more you learn about these dogs, the more equipped you will be to decide if they are the right option for you. If you decide that a Cocker Spaniel is a good fit, you will find the information you need in this book to help prepare you to become a dog owner.

If you are ready to learn more about the Cocker Spaniel breed, turn the page and keep reading!

Table of Contents

Introduction

If you were to picture a small dog with soft, wavy fur and fluffy ears, you might be picturing the Cocker Spaniel. This is a fairly old breed of dog with its origins tracing all the way back to the 14th century, but it is also one of the most popular modern breeds. What many people do not realize is that the name Cocker Spaniel actually applies to two different breeds – the American Cocker Spaniel and the English Cocker Spaniel. These breeds share much of their history but they are recognized as separate breeds by the American Kennel Club and other organizations.

The Cocker Spaniel is a small-breed dog which makes it a popular choice for condos and apartments. These dogs were developed for hunting but they make excellent companion pets as well and they generally get along well with children. Cocker Spaniels are bright and friendly little dogs but they do not require an excessive amount of exercise and they can be very happy as couch potatoes in some homes, though a daily walk is still recommended.

If you are looking for a friendly small-breed dog that makes a great family pet, consider the Cocker Spaniel. Before you decide to get one of these lovely dogs, however, you should take the time to learn as much as you can about them. Cocker Spaniels are not the right choice for everyone so you need to understand the pros and cons of the breed before you make your choice. In this book you will find a wealth of Cocker Spaniel facts and information to help you decide whether or not this is the right breed for you. If you decide that a Cocker Spaniel is a good fit, this book will help you become the best dog owner you can be.

So, if you are ready to learn more about the Cocker Spaniel breed simply turn the page and keep reading!

Glossary of Dog Terms

AKC – American Kennel Club, the largest purebred dog registry in the United States

Almond Eye – Referring to an elongated eye shape rather than a rounded shape

Apple Head – A round-shaped skull

Balance – A show term referring to all of the parts of the dog, both moving and standing, which produce a harmonious image

Beard – Long, thick hair on the dog's underjaw

Best in Show – An award given to the only undefeated dog left standing at the end of judging

Bitch – A female dog

Bite – The position of the upper and lower teeth when the dog's jaws are closed; positions include level, undershot, scissors, or overshot

Blaze – A white stripe running down the center of the face between the eyes

Board – To house, feed, and care for a dog for a fee

Breed – A domestic race of dogs having a common gene pool and characterized appearance/function

Breed Standard – A published document describing the look, movement, and behavior of the perfect specimen of a particular breed

Buff – An off-white to gold coloring

Clip – A method of trimming the coat in some breeds

Coat – The hair covering of a dog; some breeds have two coats, and outer coat and undercoat; also known as a double coat. Examples of breeds with double coats include German Shepherd, Siberian Husky, Akita, etc.

Condition – The health of the dog as shown by its skin, coat, behavior, and general appearance

Crate – A container used to house and transport dogs; also called a cage or kennel

Crossbreed (Hybrid) – A dog having a sire and dam of two different breeds; cannot be registered with the AKC

Dam (bitch) – The female parent of a dog;

Dock – To shorten the tail of a dog by surgically removing the end part of the tail.

Double Coat – Having an outer weather-resistant coat and a soft, waterproof coat for warmth; see above.

Drop Ear – An ear in which the tip of the ear folds over and hangs down; not prick or erect

Entropion – A genetic disorder resulting in the upper or lower eyelid turning in

Fancier – A person who is especially interested in a particular breed or dog sport

Fawn – A red-yellow hue of brown

Feathering – A long fringe of hair on the ears, tail, legs, or body of a dog

Groom – To brush, trim, comb or otherwise make a dog's coat neat in appearance

Heel – To command a dog to stay close by its owner's side

Hip Dysplasia – A condition characterized by the abnormal formation of the hip joint

Inbreeding – The breeding of two closely related dogs of one breed

Kennel – A building or enclosure where dogs are kept

Litter – A group of puppies born at one time

Markings – A contrasting color or pattern on a dog's coat

Mask – Dark shading on the dog's foreface

Mate – To breed a dog and a bitch

Neuter – To castrate a male dog or spay a female dog

Pads – The tough, shock-absorbent skin on the bottom of a dog's foot

Parti-Color – A coloration of a dog's coat consisting of two or more definite, well-broken colors; one of the colors must be white

Pedigree – The written record of a dog's genealogy going back three generations or more

Pied – A coloration on a dog consisting of patches of white and another color

Prick Ear – Ear that is carried erect, usually pointed at the tip of the ear

Puppy – A dog under 12 months of age

Purebred – A dog whose sire and dam belong to the same breed and who are of unmixed descent

Saddle – Colored markings in the shape of a saddle over the back; colors may vary

Shedding – The natural process whereby old hair falls off the dog's body as it is replaced by new hair growth.

Sire – The male parent of a dog

Smooth Coat – Short hair that is close-lying

Spay – The surgery to remove a female dog's ovaries, rendering her incapable of breeding

Trim – To groom a dog's coat by plucking or clipping

Undercoat – The soft, short coat typically concealed by a longer outer coat

Wean – The process through which puppies transition from subsisting on their mother's milk to eating solid food

Whelping – The act of birthing a litter of puppies

Chapter One: Understanding Cocker Spaniels

The Cocker Spaniel makes a wonderful pet, but it is not the right choice for everyone. If you think that this breed might be a good fit for you, take the time to learn everything you can. In this chapter you will find an overview of the Cocker Spaniel breed including the breed history and the two types of Cocker Spaniels. This information will help you make your decision. In the next chapter you will receive practical information about keeping Cocker Spaniel dogs that you should also consider before deciding.

Facts About Cocker Spaniels

The Cocker Spaniel is a friendly and playful breed that makes an excellent family companion as well as a talented hunting dog. While these dogs may not chase down a deer or attack a wild badger, they have a natural talent for flushing game and for retrieving. This skill comes from the breed's development from field spaniels – the Cocker Spaniel is also known for its endurance and speed, though you may not expect that from such a small dog.

In terms of size, the Cocker Spaniel ranges from about 13.5 inches to 16 inches (34 to 41 cm) depending on the sex and type – the average weight for the breed is between 24 and 32 pounds (11 to 15 kg). American Cocker Spaniels tend to be at the lower end of the spectrum for height and weight while English Cocker Spaniels are a little larger. Though this breed was developed for hunting, these dogs are not overly active or energetic. They have a moderate energy level and their exercise needs can generally be met with a 30-minute walk daily as well as some active play time.

In addition to being a talented sporting breed, the Cocker Spaniel is also a great family companion. These dogs are naturally very sweet and gentle and they can become very affectionate with family. Cocker Spaniels love to be around people and they generally do not do well when left alone for long periods of time – separation anxiety is a big problem for this breed. Because these dogs are also very smart, they require plenty of mental stimulation in addition to physical exercise. If the Cocker Spaniel gets bored, he is prone to developing problem behavior.

Some Cocker Spaniels bark more than others, but they are generally not considered to be a yappy breed. These dogs will usually bark at strangers, but they warm up fairly quickly. Cocker Spaniels get along well with other dogs and they are also good with cats and other household pets as long as they are socialized and trained from a young age. Poorly bred or improperly socialized Cocker Spaniels have a tendency to become snappy and they may be fearful of strangers as well. This is why socialization is especially important for this breed.

In addition to their sweet natures and friendly personality, Cocker Spaniels are also known for their beautiful coats. The coat for this breed is medium-length and it is very silky and fine. Cocker Spaniels can have flat or wavy coats, though curly coats are generally not preferred. Not only do their coats have some wave to them, but they also exhibit a lot of feathering on the ears, chest, abdomen, and legs. The hair tends to be a little shorter on the face and head and longer on the body, though many people trim the hair on the back to keep it manageable.

Because the Cocker Spaniel's coat grows long, regular grooming is required. You should plan to brush your dog's coat on a daily basis and keep a wide-toothed comb on hand to work through tangles. To keep your dog's coat healthy and trimmed you will also need to have him professionally groomed every 6 to 8 weeks or so. Cocker Spaniels are moderate shedders, so regular brushing and grooming will help to keep that under control as well. This breed may not be a good choice for allergy sufferers.

In terms of health, the Cocker Spaniel is a fairly healthy breed with a long lifespan averaging 12 to 15 years. One of the most common health problems seen in this breed is ear infections, due to their long and furry ears. Working Cocker Spaniels may also sustain injuries from working in the field. For major health problems, Cocker Spaniels are prone to several inherited conditions like congenital deafness, progressive retinal atrophy, glaucoma, and hip dysplasia. These dogs are also prone to allergies, autoimmune hemolytic anemia, cherry eye, epilepsy, hypothyroidism, otitis externa, and patellar luxation. Responsible breeding practices can help reduce the risk for these and other conditions.

Summary of Cocker Spaniel Facts

Pedigree: exact origins unknown, developed from field spaniels in Spain

AKC Group: Sporting Group

Breed Size: small to medium

Height: 13.5 to 16 inches (34 - 41 cm), depending on sex/type

Weight: 24 to 32 lbs. (11 to 15 kg)

Coat Length: medium-long; shorter on the head and back

Coat Texture: silky and fine; flat or wavy

Shedding: moderate, frequent grooming needed

Color: many colors and patterns; solid as well as parti-color, often with tan color points

Eyes and Nose: dark; black or brown, depending on type

Ears: drop ears; large, long and well feathered

Tail: docked short, carried horizontally

Temperament: sweet, affectionate, lively, playful, loyal, intelligent, trainable

Strangers: may bark at strangers

Children: generally good with children but should be supervised around young children

Other Dogs: generally good with other dogs if properly trained and socialized

Training: intelligent and very trainable

Exercise Needs: moderately active, does not require a great deal of exercise; 30-minute daily walk recommended

Health Conditions: allergies, autoimmune hemolytic anemia, cherry eye, congenital deafness, epilepsy, eye problems, hip dysplasia, hypothyroidism, otitis externa, and patellar luxation

Lifespan: average 12 to 15 years

Cocker Spaniel Breed History

The exact origins of the Cocker Spaniel are unknown but there are references to spaniel-type dogs dating all the way back to the 14th century. It is generally assumed that Cocker Spaniels originated in Spain, as mentions of spaniels can be found in the writings of Edward of Norwich, the 2nd Duke of York. It wasn't until the 18th century, however, that the spaniel was written about in any detail – in 1801, Sydenham Edwards wrote about the two types of "land spaniel", the hawking/springer spaniel and the cocking/cocker spaniel.

The name "cocker spaniel" comes from the breed's use in hunting the woodcock, a type of wading bird – dogs were trained to flush the birds and to retrieve them. During the 19th century, the name cocker spaniel referred generally to a type of small field spaniel and it was used for a number of breeds including those now known as the Sussex Spaniel, the Clumber Spaniel, and the Norfolk Spaniel. At the time there were also two cocker breeds – Devonshire Cockers and Welsh Cockers. These breeds were eventually recognized by the Kennel Club in 1903 as the Welsh Springer Spaniel.

Up until the 1870s there was no established standard for the Cocker Spaniel breed – the only requirement was that the dog weigh less than 25 pounds (11 kg). This weight limit was used until the early 1900s when larger specimens of the breed came to be known as Springer Spaniels. The English Cocker Spaniel was recognized as a breed by the Kennel Club in 1892 and separated from the English Springer Spaniel breed at the same time.

The founder of the modern Cocker Spaniel breed is commonly cited as the Obo Kennel run by Mr. James Farrow in England. Two of Farrow's dogs are recognized as the foundation sires of both modern Cocker Spaniel Breeds – Ch. Obo is the father of the English Cocker Spaniel while his son, Ch. Obo II, is the father of the American Cocker Spaniel. The English Cocker Spaniel was first introduced in the U.S. in the late 1870s and the American Spaniel Club was formed in 1881. It is the oldest breed club in America and, at the start, it included breeders of many types of spaniel.

It didn't take long for Cocker Spaniels to gain popularity in the United States, though selective breeding began to produce an American version of the breed. The American Cocker Spaniel was bred to be smaller than the English version. The English Cocker Spaniel Club of America was formed in 1936 and the club petitioned the AKC to prohibit the showing of American-type Cocker Spaniels in the English Cocker Spaniel class. The AKC recognized the American and English Cocker Spaniels as two separate breeds in 1946.

Types of Cocker Spaniel

As you have already learned, there are actually two separate breeds of Cocker Spaniel – the American and the English. These two breeds share their origin story up until the point when Cocker Spaniels were introduced in the United States. When this happened, breeders began developing an American type for the breed and the two breeds were eventually recognized separately by the American Kennel Club. In this section you will receive some detailed information about both breeds and what sets them apart from one another.

English Cocker Spaniel

The English Cocker Spaniel is simply known as the Cocker Spaniel in the United Kingdom because it is the breed that was originally recognized by The Kennel Club in 1982 – it was recognized by the AKC in 1946 as a separate breed from the American variety. The English Cocker Spaniel is generally a little larger than the American and its primary function is as a working breed, though there are show strains as well.

The standard height for the English Cocker Spaniel is 15.5 to 16 inches (39 to 41 cm) for an adult male and 15 to 15.5 inches (38 to 39 cm) for an adult female. The average weight of an English Cocker Spaniel for show is 28 to 32 pounds (13 to 15 kg). The English Cocker Spaniel is incredibly popular in the U.K. show circuit, having a total of seven Best in Show wins since 1928. In fact, the breed is the second most popular dog in the U.K. according to Kennel Club registration statistics – it is second to the Labrador Retriever.

The show strain for the English Cocker Spaniel is bred in adherence to The Kennel Club conformation breed standard, the working strain is bred for its working ability – this means that there are some physical differences between the two strains. The working strain typically exhibits larger, flatter heads and shorter ears – the coat is also shorter and finer with less feathering. Some say that the working strain is also more energetic than the show strain.

American Cocker Spaniel

The Cocker Spaniel was recognized by the American Kennel Club in 1878 but the two breeds were not divided into separate classes until 1935. After the division, the Cocker Spaniel Club of America began discouraging the breeding of English and American types. The American Cocker Spaniel was recognized as a separate breed by The Kennel Club until 1970. Just as the English Cocker Spaniel is simply known as the Cocker Spaniel in the U.K., the American Cocker Spaniel is known as the Cocker Spaniel in the United States.

The American version of the breed tends to be smaller than the English variety because it was developed to hunt American woodcocks – these birds are smaller than their European relatives. During the early 20th century, American breeders developed a preference for a more stylized appearance for the breed. According to the current AKC breed standard, the ideal height for the American Cocker Spaniel is 14.5 to 15.5 inches (37 to 39 cm) for adult males and 13.5 to 14.5 inches (34 to 37 cm) for adult females. The ideal weight is 24 to 30 pounds (11 to 14 kg). The American Cocker Spaniel has won Best in Show at Westminster four times and it can be shown in three different breed classes divided by color.

Chapter Two: Things to Know Before Getting a Cocker Spaniel

Now that you know a little bit more about the Cocker Spaniel breed you should have a good idea whether or not it is the right breed for you. Before you actually make your decision, however, it is important to consider the practical aspects of dog ownership. In this chapter you will receive some valuable information about licensing requirements for Cocker Spaniels as well as tips for keeping them with other dogs and household pets. You will also receive a summary of pros and cons for the breed as well as estimations for initial and monthly costs of dog ownership.

Do You Need a License?

Before purchasing a Cocker Spaniel dog, you should learn about local licensing requirements that may affect you. The licensing requirements for dog owners vary from one country to another so you may need to do a little bit of research on your own to determine whether you need a dog license or not. In the United States, there are no federal requirements for dog licensing – it is determined at the state level. While some states do not, most states require dog owners to license their dogs on an annual basis.

When you apply for a dog license you will have to submit proof that your dog has been given a rabies vaccine. Dog licenses in the United States cost about $25 (£16.25) per year and they can be renewed annually when you renew your dog's rabies vaccine. Even if your state doesn't require you to license your dog it is still a good idea because it will help someone to identify him if he gets lost so they can return him to you.

In the United Kingdom, licensing requirements for dog owners are a little bit different. The U.K. requires that all dog owners license their dogs and the license can be renewed every twelve months. The cost to license your dog in the U.K. is similar to the U.S. but you do not have to have your dog vaccinated against rabies. In fact, rabies does not exist in the U.K. because it was eradicated through careful control measures. If you travel with your dog to or from the U.K., you will have to obtain a special animal moving license and your dog may have to undergo a period of quarantine to make sure he doesn't carry disease into the country.

Do Cocker Spaniels Get Along with Other Pets?

As long as they are properly socialized, many dogs get along well with cats and other household pets – the same is true for Cocker Spaniels. Although the Cocker Spaniel was developed as a hunting breed, its primary purpose was to flush game and to retrieve it. This breed doesn't have the same prey drive that a terrier would so they are unlikely to chase cats and other small animals. It is always a good idea, however, to supervise interaction between your Cocker Spaniel and other dogs or pets.

How Many Cocker Spaniels Should You Keep?

Many people wonder whether they should keep a single dog or if they should get their dog a canine companion – especially people who work a full-time job and spend a lot of time away from home. The Cocker Spaniel is not an overly needy breed, but he does need a good deal of daily time and attention from his family. Like many breeds, the Cocker Spaniel is prone to developing behavioral problems like chewing if he spends too much time alone. These problems will be exacerbated if he also doesn't get enough exercise during the day.

Cocker Spaniels generally get along well with other dogs, though they do not necessarily need a canine companion. These dogs are very people-oriented so they will always prefer the company of family to the companionship of another dog. Still, if you are worried that you won't be able to provide for your dog's social needs each and every day, it may not be a bad idea to get another dog so they can keep each other company. Having two dogs to play together may also help to ensure that both get the daily exercise they require to work off excess energy.

How Much Does it Cost to Keep a Cocker Spaniel?

Many people do not realize that the cost to own a dog goes way beyond the purchase price of the puppy. Before you even bring your puppy home you have to think about things like buying a crate, purchasing toys and food bowls, and the cost of veterinary check-ups and vaccinations. There are also a number of recurring expenses such as your dog's license and his daily diet. Unless you are able to cover the cost to keep a dog and meet all of his needs, you should consider another type of pet. In this section you will receive an overview of the initial costs and monthly costs to keep a Cocker Spaniel.

Initial Costs

The initial costs for keeping a Cocker Spaniel include those costs that you must cover before you can bring your dog home Some of the initial costs you will need to cover include your dog's crate, food/water bowls, toys and accessories, microchipping, initial vaccinations, spay/neuter surgery and supplies for grooming and nail clipping – it also includes the cost of the dog itself. You will find an overview of each of these costs as well as an estimate for each cost on the following page:

Purchase Price – The cost to purchase a Cocker Spaniel can vary greatly depending where you find the dog. You can adopt a rescue Cocker Spaniel for as little as $200 (£180) but purchasing a puppy, especially a purebred puppy from an AKC-registered breeder, could be much more costly. The cost of a show-quality Cocker Spaniel puppy could cost as much as $2,000 (£1,800) or more. For a pet-quality puppy of good breeding, the average cost is between $800 and $1,200 (£720 - £1,080).

Crate – Because the Cocker Spaniel is a fairly small dog you will not need a very large crate and you probably won't need a different crate for when your dog is a puppy and when he is an adult. The average cost for a small dog crate is about $30 (£19.50) in most cases.

Food/Water Bowls – In addition to providing your Cocker Spaniel with a crate to sleep in, you should also make sure he has a set of high-quality food and water bowls. The best materials for these is stainless steel because it is easy to clean and doesn't harbor bacteria – ceramic is another good option. The average cost for a quality set of stainless steel bowls is about $20 (£18).

Toys – Giving your Cocker Spaniel plenty of toys to play with will help to keep him from chewing on things that are not toys – they can also be used to provide mental stimulation and enrichment. To start out, plan to buy an assortment of toys for your dog until you learn what kind he prefers. You may want to budget a cost of $50 (£45) for toys just to be sure you have enough to last through the puppy phase.

Microchipping – In the United States and United Kingdom there are no federal or state requirements saying that you have to have your dog microchipped, but it is a very good idea. Your Cocker Spaniel could slip out of his collar on a walk or lose his ID tag. If someone finds him without identification, they can take him to a shelter to have his microchip scanned. A microchip is something that is implanted under your dog's skin and it carries a number that is linked to your contact information. The procedure takes just a few minutes to perform and it only costs about $30 (£19.50) in most cases.

Initial Vaccinations – During your dog's first year of life, he will require a number of different vaccinations. If you purchase your puppy from a reputable breeder, he might already have had a few but you'll still need more over the next few months as well as booster shots each year. You should budget about $50 (£32.50) for initial vaccinations just to be prepared.

Spay/Neuter Surgery – If you don't plan to breed your Cocker Spaniel you should have him or her neutered or spayed before 6 months of age. The cost for this surgery will vary depending where you go and on the sex of your Cocker Spaniel. If you go to a traditional veterinary surgeon, the cost for spay/neuter surgery could be very high but you can save money by going to a veterinary clinic. The average cost for neuter surgery is $50 to $100 (£32.50 - £65) and spay surgery costs about $100 to $200 (£65 - £130).

Supplies/Accessories – In addition to purchasing your Cocker Spaniel's crate and food/water bowls, you should also purchase some basic grooming supplies (several brushes and a wide-toothed comb) as well as a leash and collar. The cost for these items will vary depending on the quality, but you should budget about $100 (£32.50) for these extra costs.

Initial Costs for Cocker Spaniels		
Cost	**One Dog**	**Two Dogs**
Purchase Price	$200 - $2,000 (£180 - £1,800)	$400 - $4,000 (£360 - £3,600)
Crate	$30 (£19.50)	$60 (£39)
Food/Water Bowl	$20 (£18)	$40 (£36)
Toys	$50 (£45)	$100 (£90)
Microchipping	$30 (£19.50)	$60 (£39)
Vaccinations	$50 (£32.50)	$100 (£65)
Spay/Neuter	$50 to $200 (£32.50 - £130)	$100 to $400 (£65 - £260)
Accessories	$100 (£90)	$100 (£90)
Total	$530 to $2,480 (£477 – £2,232)	$960 to $4,860 (£864 – £4,374)

*Costs may vary depending on location
**U.K. prices based on an estimated exchange of $1 = £0.90

Monthly Costs

The monthly costs for keeping a Cocker Spaniel as a pet include those costs which recur on a monthly basis. The most important monthly cost for keeping a dog is, of course, food. In addition to food, however, you'll also need to think about things like grooming costs, annual license renewal, toy replacements, and veterinary exams. You will find an

<u>overview of each of these costs as well as an estimate for each cost on the following page</u>:

Food and Treats – Feeding your Cocker Spaniel a healthy diet is very important for his health and wellness. A high-quality diet for dogs is not cheap, so you should be prepared to spend around $35 (£31.50) on a large bag of high-quality dog food which will last you at least a month. You should also include a monthly budget of about $10 (£6.50) for treats.

Grooming Costs – One of the biggest recurring expenses you will have for a Cocker Spaniel is grooming costs. The average cost for a visit to the groomer is about $50 and you should plan to have your dog groomed every 6 to 8 weeks – this means 6 to 8 visits per year. If you take an average of 7 annual visits and divide the cost evenly over 12 months you get an average cost around $30 (£27) per month.

License Renewal – The cost to license your Cocker Spaniel will generally be about $25 (£16.25) and you can renew the license for the same price each year. License renewal cost divided over 12 months is about $2 (£1.30) per month.

Veterinary Exams – In order to keep your Cocker Spaniel healthy you should take him to the veterinarian about every six months after he passes puppyhood. You might have to take him more often for the first 12 months to make sure he gets his vaccines on time. The average cost for a vet visit is about $40 (£26) so, if you have two visits per year, it averages to about $7 (£4.55) per month.

Other Costs – In addition to the monthly costs for your Cocker Spaniel's food, grooming, license renewal, and vet visits there are also some other cost you might have to pay occasionally. These costs might include things like replacements for worn-out toys, a larger collar as your puppy grows, cleaning products, and more. You should budget about $15 (£9.75) per month for extra costs.

Monthly Costs for Cocker Spaniels		
Cost	**One Dog**	**Two Dogs**
Food and Treats	$45 (£40.50)	$90 (£81)
Grooming Costs	$30 (£27)	$60 (£54)
License Renewal	$2 (£1.30)	$4 (£3.60)
Veterinary Exams	$7 (£4.55)	$14 (£12.60)
Other Costs	$15 (£9.75)	$30 (£19.50)
Total	$99 (£89)	$198 (£178)

*Costs may vary depending on location
**U.K. prices based on an estimated exchange of $1 = £0.90

What are the Pros and Cons of Cocker Spaniels?

Every pet comes with its own unique list of pros and cons – the Cocker Spaniel is no different. Before you decide whether the Cocker Spaniel might be the right pet for you, take a moment to learn the good things and the bad things about this breed. <u>You will find a list of pros and cons for the Cocker Spaniel dog breed listed below</u>:

Pros for the Cocker Spaniel Breed

- Small size and adaptable nature makes them a good choice for apartment or condo life
- Very attractive breed with silky hair and long, furry ears
- Sweet-natured temperament, generally friendly with everyone they meet
- Very devoted and loyal companions, forms close bonds with family
- Generally do not bark excessively
- Makes a great family pet and companion animal, generally gets along with children
- Usually gets along with other dogs and household pets, including cats
- Smart and trainable breed, generally responds well to positive reinforcement training methods

- Fairly long average lifespan, not prone to an excessive number of congenital health problems.
- Doesn't need a great deal of exercise though they can be trained for hunting and dog sports

Cons for the Cocker Spaniel Breed

- Has a tendency to put on weight if fed too much or if they don't get enough exercise
- Should be supervised around small children because they may not know how to handle a dog properly
- Prone to developing problem behaviors like chewing if left alone for too long
- Significant grooming is required to keep the coat in good health and condition
- Prone to developing snappy tendencies if not properly socialized from a young age
- Can be expensive to maintain with frequent grooming visits required

Chapter Three: Purchasing Cocker Spaniels

Once you have decided that the Cocker Spaniel is the right dog for you, your next step is to find one. There are many benefits to starting with a Cocker Spaniel puppy, but older rescue dogs are great as well – it is simply a matter of whether you want to deal with the "puppy phase" or not. In this chapter you will receive valuable information about finding a Cocker Spaniel breeder or rescue. You will also receive tips for picking out a healthy Cocker Spaniel puppy and for puppy-proofing your home.

Where Can You Buy Cocker Spaniels?

If you are sure that a Cocker Spaniel is right for you, you need to start thinking about where you are going to get your new dog. Many people think that the best place to find a dog is at the pet store but, unfortunately, they are greatly mistaken. While the puppies at the pet store might look cute and cuddly, there is no way to know whether they are actually healthy or well-bred. Many pet stores get their puppies from puppy mills and they sell the puppies to unsuspecting dog lovers. Puppy mill puppies are often already sick by the time they make it to the pet store, often traveling across state lines to get there.

A puppy mill is a type of breeding facility that focuses on breeding and profit more than the health and wellbeing of the dogs. Puppy mills usually keep their dogs in squalid conditions, forcing them to bear litter after litter of puppies with little to no rest in between. Many of the breeders used in puppy mills are poorly bred themselves or unhealthy to begin with which just ensures that the puppies will have the same problems. The only time you should bring home a puppy from a pet store is if the store has a partnership with a local shelter and that is where they get their dogs. If the pet store can't tell you which breeder the puppies came from, or if they don't offer you any paperwork or registration for the puppy, it is likely that the puppy came from a puppy mill.

Rather than purchasing a Cocker Spaniel puppy from a pet store, your best bet is to find a reputable Cocker Spaniel breeder – preferably and AKC-registered breeder in the United States or a Kennel Club-registered breeder in the U.K. If you visit the website for either of these organizations you can find a list of breeders for all of the club-recognized breeds. You can also look for breeders on the website for other breed clubs like the American Cocker Spaniel Club or the UK Cocker Spaniel Club. Even if these organizations don't provide a list of breeders you may be able to speak with members to find information.

If you don't have your heart set on a Cocker Spaniel puppy, consider adopting a rescue from a local shelter. There are many benefits associated with rescuing an adult dog. For one thing, adoption fees are generally under $200 (£180) which is much more affordable than the $800 to $1,200 (£720 to £1,080) fee to buy a puppy from a breeder. Plus, an adult dog will already be housetrained and may have some obedience training as well. As an added bonus, most shelters spay/neuter their dogs before adopting them out so you won't have to pay for the surgery yourself. Another benefit is that an adult dog has already surpassed the puppy stage so his personality is set – with a puppy you can never quite be sure how your puppy will turn out.

If you are thinking about adopting a Cocker Spaniel, consider one of these breed-specific rescues:

United States Rescues:

Oldies But Goodies Cocker Rescue.
<http://www.cockerspanielrescue.com/>

Cocker Spaniel Rescue of New England, Inc.
<http://csrne.org/>

Cocker Spaniel Adoption Center, Inc.
<http://www.cockeradoptions.org/Public/Default.aspx>

Cherished Cockers Rescue. <http://cherishedcockers.org/>

Cockers Across PA Cocker Spaniel Rescue, Inc.
<http://www.cockersacrosspa.org/>

You can also find a list of Cocker Spaniels in need of homes using the Cocker Spaniel Rescue Network directory. <http://www.cockerspanielrescue.org/>

United Kingdom Rescues:

Cocker & English Springer Spaniel Rescue.
<http://www.caessr.org.uk/>

The Cocker Spaniel Club of Scotland.
<http://www.cockerspanielclubofscotland.co.uk/cocker-rescue/>

Working Cocker Spaniel Rescue.
<http://www.workingcockerspanielrescue.co.uk/>

The Cocker Spaniel Club Rescue.
<http://www.thecockerspanielclub.co.uk/rescue.htm>

You may also be able to find Cocker Spaniel rescues using the UK Kennel Club rescue directory:
<http://www.thekennelclub.org.uk/services/public/findaresc ue/Default.aspx?breed=2052 >

How to Choose a Reputable Cocker Spaniel Breeder

When you are ready to start looking for a Cocker Spaniel puppy you may begin your search for a breeder online. A simple internet search will probably give you a variety of results but, if you want to find a reputable breeder, you may have to dig a little deeper. Compile a list of breeders from whatever sources you can and then take the time to go through each option to determine whether the breeder is reputable and responsible or not. You do not want to run the risk of purchasing a puppy from a hobby breeder or from someone who doesn't follow responsible breeding practices. If you aren't careful about where you get your

Cocker Spaniel puppy you could end up with a puppy that is already sick.

Once you have your list of breeders on hand you can go through them one-by-one to narrow down your options. Go through the following steps to do so:

- Visit the website for each breeder on your list (if they have one) and look for key information about the breeder's history and experience.
  - o Check for club registrations and a license, if applicable.
  - o If the website doesn't provide any information about the facilities or the breeder you are best just moving on.
- After ruling out some of the breeders, contact the remaining breeders on your list by phone
  - o Ask the breeder questions about his experience with breeding dogs in general and about the Cocker Spaniel breed in particular.
  - o Ask for information about the breeding stock including registration numbers and health information.
  - o Expect a reputable breeder to ask you questions about yourself as well – a responsible breeder wants to make sure that his puppies go to good homes.

- Schedule an appointment to visit the facilities for the remaining breeders on your list after you've weeded a few more of them out.
    - o Ask for a tour of the facilities, including the place where the breeding stock is kept as well as the facilities housing the puppies.
    - o If things look unorganized or unclean, do not purchase from the breeder.
    - o Make sure the breeding stock is in good condition and that the puppies are all healthy-looking and active.
- Narrow down your list to a final few options and then interact with the puppies to make your decision.
    - o Make sure the breeder provides some kind of health guarantee and ask about any vaccinations the puppies may have already received.
- Put down a deposit, if needed, to reserve a puppy if they aren't ready to come home yet.

Tips for Selecting a Healthy Cocker Spaniel Puppy

After you have narrowed down your options for breeders you then need to pick out your puppy. If you are a first-time dog owner, do not let yourself become caught up in the excitement of a new puppy – take the time to make a careful selection. If you rush the process you could end up with a puppy that isn't healthy or one whose personality isn't compatible with your family. <u>Follow the steps below to pick out your Cocker Spaniel puppy</u>:

- Ask the breeder to give you a tour of the facilities, especially where the puppies are kept.
  - Make sure the facilities where the puppies are housed is clean and sanitary – if there is evidence of diarrhea, do not purchase one of the puppies because they may already be sick.
- Take a few minutes to observe the litter as a whole, watching how the puppies interact with each other.
  - The puppies should be active and playful, interacting with each other in a healthy way.
  - Avoid puppies that appear to be lethargic and those that have difficulty moving – they could be sick.
- Approach the litter and watch how the puppies react to you when you do.
  - If the puppies appear frightened they may not be properly socialized and you do not want a puppy like that.
  - The puppies may be somewhat cautious, but they should be curious and interested in you.

- Let the puppies approach you and give them time to sniff and explore you before you interact with them.
    - Pet the puppies and encourage them to play with a toy, taking the opportunity to observe their personalities.
    - Single out any of the puppies that you think might be a good fit and spend a little time with them.
- Pick up the puppy and hold him to see how he responds to human contact.
    - The puppy might squirm a little but it shouldn't be frightened of you and it should enjoy being pet.
- Examine the puppy's body for signs of illness and injury
    - The puppy should have clear, bright eyes with no discharge. The coat should be even and bright white, no patches of hair loss or discoloration.
    - The ears should be clean and clear with no discharge or inflammation.
    - The puppy's stomach may be round but it shouldn't be distended or swollen.
    - The puppy should be able to walk and run normally without any mobility problems.
- Narrow down your options and choose the puppy that you think is the best fit.

Once you've chosen your puppy, ask the breeder about the next steps. Do not take the puppy home if it isn't at least 8 weeks old and unless it has been fully weaned and eating solid food.

Puppy-Proofing Your Home

After you've picked out your Cocker Spaniel puppy you may still have to wait a few weeks until you can bring him home. During this time you should take steps to prepare your home, making it a safe place for your puppy. The process of making your home safe for your puppy is called "puppy proofing" and it involves removing or storing away anything and everything that could harm your puppy. It might help for you to crawl around the house on your hands and knees, viewing things from your puppy's perspective.

<u>On the following page you will find a list of things you should do when you are puppy-proofing your home</u>:

- Make sure your trash and recycling containers have a tight-fitting lid or store them in a cabinet.

- Put away all open food containers and keep them out of reach of your puppy.

- Store cleaning products and other hazardous chemicals in a locked cabinet or pantry where your puppy can't get them.

- Make sure electrical cords and blind pulls are wrapped up and placed out of your puppy's reach.

- Pick up any small objects or toys that could be a choking hazard if your puppy chews on them.

- Cover or drain any open bodies of water such as the toilet, and outdoor pond, etc.

- Store any medications and beauty products in the medicine cabinet out of your puppy's reach.

- Check your home for any plants that might be toxic to dogs and remove them or put them out of reach.

- Block off fire places, windows, and doors so your puppy can't get into trouble.

- Close off any stairwells and block the entry to rooms where you do not want your puppy to be.

Chapter Four: Caring for Cocker Spaniels

Now that you know a little more about the practical aspects of keeping a Cocker Spaniel as a pet you are ready to learn the details that will be involved in your task as a dog owner. In this chapter you will learn about the habitat and exercise requirements of the Cocker Spaniel and receive some tips for making your new puppy feel at home. By ensuring that your puppy has a space to call his own you will have a way to keep him confined in your absence without always keeping him in a crate.

Habitat and Exercise Requirements for Cocker Spaniel

The Cocker Spaniel is a small-breed dog so they do not require a lot of space but they can be fairly active dogs in some cases. Even if your Cocker Spaniel doesn't need a lot of space, however, he still needs enough exercise to work off excess energy. If you live in an urban area, you might not have a backyard where your Cocker Spaniel can play. In cases like his, regular exercise is incredibly important – you'll need to take your dog on a daily walk for at least 30 minutes. You can also give your Cocker Spaniel exercise by training him for hunting, field trials, or other dog sports.

To make your Cocker Spaniel comfortable and to ensure that he feels at-home, you will need to provide him with certain things. A crate is one of the most important things you will need when you bring your new Cocker Spaniel puppy home. Not only will it be a place for your puppy to sleep, but it will also be a place where you can confine him during the times when you are away from home or when you cannot keep a close eye on him. Your puppy will also need some other basic things like a water bowl, a food bowl, a collar, a leash, toys, and grooming supplies.

When shopping for food and water bowls, safety and sanitation are the top two considerations. Stainless steel is the best material to go with because it is easy to clean and resistant to bacteria. Ceramic is another good option, though it may be a little heavier. Avoid plastic food and water bowls because they can become scratched and the scratches may harbor bacteria. For your dog's collar and leash, choose one that is appropriate to his size. This may mean that you will purchase several collars and leashes while your puppy is still growing. You might also consider a harness – this will be helpful during leash training because it will improve your control over your puppy and it will distribute pressure across his back instead of putting it all on his throat.

Provide your Cocker Spaniel puppy with an assortment of different toys and let him figure out which ones he likes. Having a variety of toys around the house is very important because you'll need to use them to redirect your puppy's natural chewing behavior as he learns what he is and is not allowed to chew on. As for grooming supplies, you'll need a wire-pin brush for daily brushing as well as a slicker brush to work through tangles. You might also want a metal comb with wide teeth that you can use to work through stubborn mats and tangles.

Setting Up Your Puppy's Area

Before you bring your Cocker Spaniel puppy home, you should set up a particular area in your home for him to call his own. The ideal setup will include your puppy's crate, a comfy dog bed, his food and water bowls, and an assortment of toys. You can arrange all of these items in a small room that is easy to block off or you can use a puppy playpen to give your puppy some free space while still keeping him somewhat confined.

When you bring your puppy home you'll have to work with him a little bit to get him used to the crate. It is very important that you do this because you do not want your puppy to form a negative association with the crate.

You want your puppy to learn that the crate is his own special place, a place where he can go to relax and take a nap if he wants to. If you use the crate as punishment, your puppy will not want to use it.

To get your puppy used to the crate, try tossing a few treats into it and let him go fish them out. Feeding your puppy his meals in the crate with the door open will be helpful as well. You can also incorporate the crate into your playtime, tossing toys into the crate or hiding treats under a blanket in the crate. As your puppy gets used to the crate you can start keeping him in it with the door closed for short periods of time, working your way up to longer periods. Just be sure to let your puppy outside before and after you confine him and never force him to stay in the crate for longer than he is physically capable of holding his bowels and his bladder.

Chapter Five: Meeting Your Cocker Spaniel's Nutritional Needs

One of the most important things you can do to ensure that your Cocker Spaniel has a long and happy life is to provide him with a wholesome and nutritious diet. The nutritional needs of dogs are different from those of humans, so take the time to learn what they are and how to meet them before you bring your puppy home. In this chapter you will learn about the basic nutritional needs of dogs and receive specific feeding tips for the Cocker Spaniel breed to help you give your puppy a long, happy life.

The Nutritional Needs of Dogs

Like all mammals, dogs require a balance of protein, carbohydrate and fat in their diets – this is in addition to essential vitamins and minerals. It is important to understand, however, that your dog's nutritional needs are very different from your own. For dogs, protein is the most important nutritional consideration followed by fat and then carbohydrates. In order to keep your dog healthy you need to create a diet that provides the optimal levels of these three macronutrients.

The portion of your dog's diet that comes from protein should be made up of animal sources like meat, poultry, and fish as well as meat meals. Protein is made up of amino acids which are the building blocks that make up your dog's tissues and cells. It also provides some energy for your dog. The most highly concentrated type of energy your Cocker Spaniel needs, however, is fat. This nutrient is particularly important for small-breed dogs because they have very fast metabolisms and therefore very high needs for energy.

Consider this – small-breed dogs have higher needs for calories by bodyweight than large dogs. A large-breed dog like a 110-pound Akita, for example, might need a total daily calorie intake of 2,500 calories, but that only amounts to about 23 calories per pound of bodyweight. A 22-pound Cocker Spaniel, on the other hand, might only need 750 calories per day but that equates to about 34 calories per pound of its total bodyweight. A significant portion of these calories needs to come from fat in order to meet your dog's nutritional needs.

In addition to protein and fat, your Cocker Spaniel also needs carbohydrates to provide dietary fiber and various vitamins and minerals. Dogs do not have a specific need for carbohydrates but they should always come from digestible sources since a dog's digestive tract is not designed to process plant foods as effectively as protein and fat. Your dog also needs plenty of fresh water on a daily basis as well as key vitamins and minerals.

How to Select a High-Quality Dog Food Brand

Shopping for dog food can be difficult for some dog owners simply because there are so many different options to choose from. If you walk into your local pet store you will see multiple aisles filled with bags of dog food from different brands and most brands offer a number of different formulas. So how do you choose a healthy dog food for your Cocker Spaniel?

The best place to start when shopping for dog food is to read the dog food label. Pet food in the United States is loosely regulated by the American Association of Feed Control Officials (AAFCO) and they evaluate commercial dog food products according to their ability to meet the basic nutritional needs of dogs in various life stages. If the product meets these basic needs, the label will carry some kind of statement from AAFCO like this:

"[Product Name] is formulated to meet the nutritional levels established by the AAFCO Dog Food nutrient profiles for [Life Stage]."

If the dog food product you are looking at contains this statement you can move on to reading the ingredients list. Dog food labels are organized in descending order by volume. This means that the ingredients at the top of the list are used in higher quantities than the ingredients at the end of the list. This being the case, you want to see high-quality sources of animal protein at the beginning of the list. Things like fresh meat, poultry or fish are excellent ingredients but they contain about 80% water. After the product is cooked, the actual volume and protein content of the ingredient will be less. Meat meals (like chicken meal or salmon meal) have already been cooked down so they contain up to 300% more protein by weight than fresh meats.

In addition to high-quality animal proteins, you want to check the ingredients list for digestible carbohydrates and healthy fats. For dogs, digestible carbohydrates include things like brown rice and oatmeal, as long as they have been cooked properly. You can also look for gluten-free and grain-free options like sweet potato and tapioca. It is best to avoid products that are made with corn, wheat, or soy ingredients because they are low in nutritional value and may trigger food allergies in your dog.

In terms of fat, you want to see at least one animal source such as chicken fat or salmon oil. Plant-based fats like flaxseed and canola oil are not necessarily bad, but they are less biologically valuable for your dog. If they are accompanied by an animal source of fat, it is okay. Just make sure that the fats included in the recipe provide a blend of both omega-3 and omega-6 fatty acids. This will help to preserve the quality and condition of your Maltese dog's skin and coat.

In addition to checking the ingredients list for beneficial ingredients you should also know that there are certainly things you do NOT want to see listed. Avoid products made with low-quality fillers like corn gluten meal or rice bran – you should also avoid artificial colors, flavors, and preservatives. Some commonly used artificial preservatives are BHA and BHT. In most cases the label will tell you if natural preservatives are used.

Tips for Feeding Your Cocker Spaniel

Cocker Spaniels are one of many breeds that are prone to obesity with overfeeding – this is especially true for dogs that do not get enough exercise. The Cocker Spaniel is a fairly active breed by nature and they were developed for hunting so their bodies are built to run. If your dog spends his whole day lying on the couch, however, his calorie needs will be much lower than a Cocker Spaniel who is training for field trials or hunting. To make sure your Cocker Spaniel doesn't get too many calories, feed him a balanced adult dog formula or consider a healthy weight formula if he is carrying a few extra pound. Conversely, if your Cocker Spaniel is in training he may need an active dog formula to provide for his additional energy requirements.

Once you've chosen a healthy diet for your Cocker Spaniel dog you need to know how much and how often to feed him. Because different dog food products have different calorie content you should follow the feeding instructions on the label as a starting point. Most dog food labels provide feeding instructions by weight, so make sure you know how much your dog weighs. It is also important to remember that these are feeding suggestions – you might have to alter the ration for your dog. If your Cocker Spaniel starts to gain too much weight, decrease his daily ration a little. If he loses weight, increase it a little bit.

In addition to knowing how much to feed your Cocker Spaniel you also need to think about how often to feed him. Most dog owners recommend feeding your dog twice a day. Small-breed dogs like the Cocker Spaniel have very fast metabolisms, however, so you might want to divide his daily portion over three small meals. As your puppy is growing you can feed him freely, allowing him to eat as much as he wants. Once he reaches full size, though, you should start rationing his food.

Dangerous Foods to Avoid

It might be tempting to give in to your dog when he is begging at the table, but certain "people foods" can actually be toxic for your dog. As a general rule, you should never feed your dog anything unless you are 100% sure that it is safe. <u>Below you will find a list of foods that can be toxic to dogs and should therefore be avoided</u>:

- Alcohol
- Apple seeds
- Avocado
- Cherry pits
- Chocolate
- Coffee

- Garlic
- Grapes/raisins
- Hops
- Macadamia nuts
- Mold
- Mushrooms

- Mustard seeds
- Onions/leeks
- Peach pits
- Potato leaves/stems
- Rhubarb leaves
- Tea
- Tomato leaves/stems
- Walnuts
- Xylitol
- Yeast dough

If your Cocker Spaniel eats any of these foods, contact the Pet Poison Control hotline right away at (888) 426 – 4435.

Chapter Six: Training Your Cocker Spaniel

Aside from making sure that your Cocker Spaniel's basic needs are met, your biggest responsibility as a dog owner is to train him. Dog training is not as complicated as many people think – it just requires time, dedication, and consistency. In this chapter you will learn the basics about socializing your new Cocker Spaniel puppy and receive tips for crate training and obedience training. Because Cocker Spaniels are an intelligent breed they take readily to training – just be as consistent as possible in issuing praise and rewards to reinforce good behavior.

Socializing Your New Cocker Spaniel Puppy

The first three months of life is when your Cocker Spaniel puppy will be the most impressionable. This is when you need to socialize him because the experiences he has as a puppy will shape the way he interacts with the world as an adult. If you don't properly socialize your Cocker Spaniel puppy then he could grow up to be a mal-adjusted adult who fears new experiences. Some Cocker Spaniels even become snappy around strangers when they are not properly socialized. Fortunately, socialization is very simple – all you have to do is make sure that your puppy has plenty of new experiences. <u>Below you will find a list of things you should expose your puppy to for properly socialization</u>:

- Introduce your puppy to friends in the comfort of your own home.

- Invite friends with dogs or puppies to come meet your Cocker Spaniel (make sure everyone is vaccinated).

- Expose your puppy to people of different sizes, shapes, gender, and skin color.

- Introduce your puppy to children of different ages – just make sure they know how to handle the puppy safely.

- Take your puppy with you in the car when you run errands.

- Walk your puppy in as many places as possible so he is exposed to different surfaces and surroundings.

- Expose your puppy to water from hoses, sprinklers, showers, pools, etc.

- Make sure your puppy experiences loud noises such as fireworks, cars backfiring, loud music, thunder, etc.

- Introduce your puppy to various appliances and tools such as blenders, lawn mowers, vacuums, etc.

- Walk your puppy with different types of harnesses, collars, and leashes.

- Once he is old enough, take your puppy to the dog park to interact with other dogs.

Positive Reinforcement for Obedience Training

Training a dog is not as difficult as many people think – it all has to do with the rewards. Think about this – if you want someone do so something for you, you probably offer them something in return. The same concept is true for dog training – if you reward your dog for performing a particular behavior then he will be more likely to repeat it in the future. This is called positive reinforcement training and it is one of the simplest yet most effective training methods you can use as a dog owner.

The key to success with dog training is two-fold. For one thing, you need to make sure that your dog understands what it is you are asking him. If he doesn't know what a command means it doesn't matter how many times you say it, he won't respond correctly. In order to teach your dog what a command means you should give it and then guide him to perform the behavior. Once he does, immediately give him a treat and praise him – the sooner you reward after identifying the desired behavior, the faster your puppy will learn.

The second key to success in dog training is consistency. While your puppy is learning basic obedience commands you need to use the same commands each and every time and you need to be consistent in rewarding him. If you maintain consistency it should only take a few repetitions for your puppy to learn what you expect of him. You can then move on to another command and alternate between them to reinforce your puppy's understanding. Just be sure to keep your training sessions short – about 15 minutes – so your puppy doesn't get bored.

Crate Training - Housebreaking Your Puppy

In addition to obedience training, house training is very important for puppies. After all, you don't want to spend your dog's entirely life following after him with a pooper scooper. The key to house training is to use your puppy's crate appropriately. When you are able to watch your puppy, keep him in the same room with you at all times and take him outdoors once every hour or so to give him a chance to do his business. Always lead him to a particular section of the yard and give him a command like "Go pee" so he learns what is expected of him when you take him to this area.

When you can't watch your puppy and overnight you should confine him to his crate. The crate should be just large enough for your puppy to stand up, sit down, turn around and lie down in. Keeping it this size will ensure that he views the crate as his den and he will be reluctant to soil it. Just make sure that you don't keep your puppy in the crate for longer than he is physically capable of holding his bladder. Always take your puppy out before putting him in the crate and immediately after releasing him.

If you give your puppy ample opportunity to do his business outdoors and you keep him confined to the crate when you can't watch him, housetraining should only take a few weeks. Again, consistency is key here so always reward and praise your puppy for doing his business outside so he learns to do it that way. If your puppy does have an accident, do not punish him because he will not understand – he won't associate the punishment with the crime so he will just learn to fear you instead.

Chapter Seven: Grooming Your Cocker Spaniel Properly

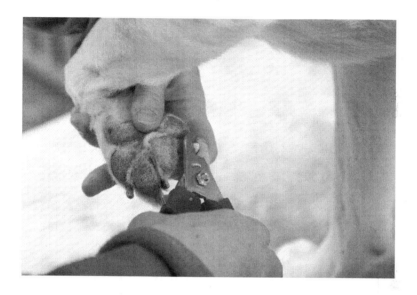

In addition to taking care of your dog's body with a healthy diet and developing his mind with regular exercise and training, you also need to take care of his coat. Cocker Spaniel's have medium-length coats of fine, silky hair that often develops a wave. Due to the length and thickness of the dog's coat, regular brushing and grooming is recommended. In this chapter you will receive some tips for grooming your Cocker Spaniel as well as information about other important tasks like ear cleaning and nail trimming.

Recommended Tools to Have on Hand

If you plan to groom your Cocker Spaniel yourself you will need certain tools and supplies. Even if you choose to have your dog professionally groomed, you should still have some supplies available for daily brushing and occasional bathing. <u>You will find a list of several recommended grooming tools and supplies below</u>:

- Wire-pin brush
- Metal wide-tooth comb
- Slicker brush (or undercoat rake)
- Small, sharp scissors
- Dog-friendly shampoo
- Nail clippers
- Dog-friendly ear cleaning solution
- Dog toothbrush
- Dog-friendly toothpaste

Tips for Bathing and Grooming Cocker Spaniels

Because Cocker Spaniels can develop thick, wavy coats, you may want to have it cleaned and trimmed by a professional groomer. Even if you do, however, you will still need to brush your dog's coat on a daily basis to prevent mats and tangles. Brushing your Cocker Spaniel's coat is very easy but it will take some time– just start at the base of the neck and work your way along the dog's back, down his legs, and under his belly. Always brush in the direction of hair growth and move slowly so you don't hurt your dog if you come across a snag.

If you encounter a mat or a tangle while brushing your Cocker Spaniel, try using a wide-toothed comb to gently work through it. The more frequently you brush your Cocker Spaniel, the less likely he is to develop mats and tangles. If you can't work the tangle out, you may need to cut it out of your dog's coat. Take a pair of sharp scissors in one hand and pinch the hair at the base of the mat (between the dog's skin and the mat) with your other hand – cut through the hairs a few at a time while gently pulling on the mat until it comes free.

Because of their long, wavy coats, Cocker Spaniels tend to attract dirt and dust. If you need to bathe your Cocker Spaniel you will want to brush him first. When you are ready for the bath, fill the bathtub with a few inches of warm (not hot) water and place your dog inside. Use a cup to pour water over your dog's back or use a handheld sprayer to wet down his coat. Once your dog's coat is dampened, apply a small amount of dog-friendly shampoo and work it into a lather. After shampooing, rinse your dog's coat thoroughly to get rid of all the soap and then towel him dry. If it is warm you might be able to let his coat air-dry but if it is cold you should finish it off with a blow dryer on the low heat setting.

While you might be able to handle brushing and bathing your Cocker Spaniel yourself, trimming his coat is probably best left to the professionals. There are several different clips that Cocker Spaniel owners tend to prefer. If you plan to show your dog you should go with the standard cut which does not actually involve any major trimming except for the fur on the feet to keep them neat – the groomer may also trim the fur on your dog's back to enhance his natural lines. If your Cocker Spaniel is only being kept as a pet, you can feel free to keep his fur trimmed a little shorter – this will help to prevent mats and tangles, also keeping his coat smoother between brushings. If you want to trim your dog's coat yourself, ask the groomer to show you how to do it before you try it at home.

Other Grooming Tasks

In addition to brushing and bathing your Cocker Spaniel, you also need to engage in some other grooming tasks including trimming your dog's nails, cleaning his ears, and brushing his teeth. You will find an overview of each of these grooming tasks below:

Trimming Your Dog's Nails

Your dog's nails grow in the same way that your own nails grow so they need to be trimmed occasionally. Most down owners find that trimming their dog's nails once a week or twice a month is sufficient. Before you trim your Cocker Spaniel's nails for the first time you should have your veterinarian or a professional groomer show you how to do it. A dog's nail contains a quick – the blood vessel that supplies blood to the nail – and if you cut the nail too short you could sever it. A severed quick will cause your dog pain and it will bleed profusely. The best way to avoid cutting your dog's nails too short is to just trim the sharp tip.

Cleaning Your Dog's Ears

The Cocker Spaniel has drop ears which means that they hang down on either side of the dog's head – they are also fairly large and covered in fur. This, combined with the fact that most dogs have hair inside their ears as well, increases the dog's risk for ear infections. If the dog's ears get wet it creates an environment that is beneficial for infection-causing bacteria. Keeping your dog's ears clean and dry is the key to preventing infections. If you have to clean your dog's ears, use a dog ear cleaning solution and squeeze a few drops into the ear canal. Then, massage the base of your dog's ears to distribute the solution then wipe it away using a clean cotton ball.

Brushing Your Dog's Teeth

Many dog owners neglect their dog's dental health which is a serious mistake. Small-breed dogs like the Cocker Spaniel have a high risk for dental problems because their mouths are so small and their teeth can become overcrowded. You should brush your dog's teeth with a dog-friendly toothbrush and dog toothpaste to preserve his dental health. Feeing your dog dental treats and giving him hard rubber toys can also help to maintain his dental health.

Chapter Eight: Breeding Cocker Spaniels

When you hold your Cocker Spaniel puppy for the first time it is easy to be tempted by the idea of breeding dogs so you will have an endless supply of puppies to play with. Breeding dogs is not a decision that should be taken lightly, however – it can be dangerous for the dog and it is a big responsibility to care for a pregnant dog and a litter of puppies. In this chapter you will learn the ins and outs of breeding Cocker Spaniels so you can decide whether it is really the right choice for you and your dog. If you think that it is, you will have the information you need to get started on the right track.

Basic Dog Breeding Information

Before you decide whether or not to breed your Cocker Spaniel, you should take the time to learn the basics about dog breeding in general. If you do not want to breed your dog, the ASPCA recommends having him neutered or her spayed before the age of 6 months. For female dogs, six months is around the time the dog experiences her first heat. Heat is just another name for the estrus cycle in dogs and it generally lasts for about 14 to 21 days. The frequency of heat may vary slightly from one dog to another but it generally occurs twice a year. When your female dog goes into heat, this is when she is capable of becoming pregnant.

If you do plan to breed your Cocker Spaniel, it is important that you wait until she reaches sexual maturity. Your dog may be full-size by the time she reaches one year of age, but most Cocker Spaniel breeders recommend waiting until she is two years old to breed her. Not only does this ensure that the dog is mature enough to physically carry and bear a litter, but it also provides enough time for any serious health problems to develop. If the dog does display signs of congenital health problems, she should not be bred for fear of passing them on. It is also important not to breed your Cocker Spaniel after the age of 8 – she may still be capable of breeding but it is not in her best interests to put that much stress on her body once she becomes a senior dog.

In addition to making sure that your Cocker Spaniels are the right age for breeding, you also have to be careful about choosing the right pairing. You should only breed Cocker Spaniels if your goal is to preserve or improve the breed – it should not be done for selfish reasons such as to make money. If you do breed these dogs you need to make sure that both the male and female are good examples of the breed standard and that you breed them in such a way as to preserve that standard. This means that you should only breed solid-color Cocker Spaniels to solid-colored dogs and parti-colored to parti-colored dogs. Mixing solid and parti-colored dogs will result in mismarking.

Once you've made sure that you have chosen the ideal breeding pair you can start to think about the details of heat and breeding. When a female dog goes into heat there are a few common signs you can look for. The first sign of heat is swelling of the vulva – this may be accompanied by a bloody discharge. Over the course of the heat cycle the discharge lightens in color and becomes more watery. By the 10th day of the cycle the discharge is light pink – this is when she begins to ovulate and it is when she is most fertile. If you plan to breed your Cocker Spaniel, this is when you want to introduce her to the male dog. If the isn't receptive to the male's advances, wait a day or two before trying again.

A dog is technically capable of conceiving at any point during the heat cycle because the male's sperm can survive in her reproductive tract for up to 5 days. If you don't plan to breed your Cocker Spaniel you need to keep her locked away while she is in heat. A male dog can smell a female dog in heat from several miles away and an intact male dog will go to great lengths to breed. Never take a female dog in heat to the dog park and be very careful about taking her outside at all. Do not leave her unattended in your backyard because a stray dog could get in and breed with her.

If you want to breed your Cocker Spaniel you will need to keep track of her estrus cycle so you know when to breed her. It generally takes a few years for a dog's cycle to become regular and some small-breed dogs go into heat more than twice per year. Keep track of your dog's cycle on a calendar so you know when to breed her. Tracking her cycle and making note of when you introduce her to the male dog will help you predict the due date for the puppies. Once you do start breeding your dog, be sure to skip at least one heat cycle between litters – ideally, you should give your dog a year to rest between litters.

Breeding Tips and Raising Puppies

After the male dog fertilizes the egg inside the female's body, the female will go through the gestation period during which the puppies start to develop inside her womb. The gestation period for Cocker Spaniel dogs lasts for anywhere from 61 to 65 days with the average being 63. However, you won't be able to actually tell that your dog is pregnant until after the third week. By the 25th day of pregnancy it is safe for a vet to perform an ultrasound and by day 28 he should be able to feel the puppies by palpating the female's abdomen. At the six week mark an x-ray can be performed to check the size of the litter. The average litter size for Cocker Spaniels is between 1 and 7 puppies, though 5 or 6 is the average.

While the puppies are growing inside your female dog's belly you need to take careful care of her. You don't need to feed your dog any extra until the fourth or fifth week of pregnancy when she really starts to gain weight. Make sure to provide your dog with a healthy diet and keep up with regular vet appointments to make sure the pregnancy is progressing well. Once you reach the fifth week of pregnancy you can increase your dog's daily rations in proportion to her weight gain.

After eight weeks of gestation you should start to get ready for your Cocker Spaniel to give birth – in dogs, this is called whelping. You should provide your dog with a clean, safe, and quiet place to give birth such as a large box in a dimly lit room. Line the box with old towels or newspapers for easy cleanup after the birth and make sure your dog has access to the box at all times. As she nears her due date she will start spending more and more time in the box.

When your Cocker Spaniel is ready to give birth her internal temperature will decrease slightly. If you want to predict when the puppies will be born you can start taking her internal temperature once a day during the last week of gestation. When the dog's body temperature drops from 100°F to 102°F (37.7°C to 38.8°C to about 98°F (36.6°C), labor is likely to begin very soon. At this point your dog will display obvious signs of discomfort such as pacing, panting, or changing positions. Just let her do her own thing but keep an eye on her in case of complications.

During the early stages of labor, your Cocker Spaniel will experience contractions about 10 minutes apart. If she has contractions for more than 2 hours without giving birth, bring her to the vet immediately. Once your Maltese starts whelping, she will whelp one puppy about every thirty minutes. After every puppy is born, she will clean it with her tongue – this will also help stimulate the puppy to start breathing on its own. After all of the puppies have been born, the mother will expel the afterbirth and the puppies will begin nursing.

It is essential that the puppies start nursing as soon as possible after whelping so that they get the colostrum. The colostrum is the first milk a mother produces and it is loaded with nutrients as well as antibodies that will protect the puppies while their own immune systems continue developing. The puppies will generally start nursing on their own or the mother will encourage them. After the puppies nurse for a little while you should make sure that your mother dog eats something as well.

When they are first born, Cocker Spaniel puppies are very small – they may only weigh about 8 to 8.5 ounces (250 grams). Over the next week they will grow to 14.5 ounces (410g) and they will continue growing over the next several months until they zone in on their adult size. It is a good idea to weigh the puppies once a week or so to make sure they are growing at a healthy rate. When Cocker Spaniel puppies are born they will have some very fine hair but it isn't enough to keep them warm – your mother dog will help with that. The puppies will be born with their eyes and ears closed but they will start to open around the second or third week following birth.

Your Cocker Spaniel puppies will be heavily dependent on their mother for the first few weeks of life until they start becoming more mobile. Around 5 to 6 weeks of age you should start offering your puppies small amounts of solid food soaked in broth or water to start the weaning process. Over the next few weeks the puppies will start to nurse less and eat more solid food. Around 8 weeks of age they should be completely weaned – this is when they are ready to be separated from their mother.

Chapter Nine: Tips for Showing Your Cocker Spaniel

One of the greatest pleasures of keeping a purebred dog is the challenge of participating in a dog show. Cocker Spaniels are a very attractive breed that tends to do well in conformation shows but they can also participate in field trials and other dog sports. If you hope to show your Cocker Spaniel, be sure to purchase a puppy from an AKC-registered breeder and check to see that your dog is a good example of the breed standard before you sign him up. In this chapter you will receive an overview of the breed standards for both Cocker Spaniel breeds.

American Cocker Spaniel Breed Standard

The AKC breed standard for the Cocker Spaniel breed provides guidelines for both breeding and showing. AKC-registered breeders must select dogs that adhere to the standards of the breed and all Cocker Spaniel owners who seek to show their dogs at AKC shows must compare them to the official breed standard as well. <u>Below you will find an overview of the breed standard for the American Cocker Spaniel breed</u>:

General Appearance and Temperament

The American Cocker Spaniel is a small dog with a sturdy and compact build, well-muscled, and capable of great speed and endurance. The breed is even-tempered with no suggestion of timidity.

Head and Neck

The head is well-proportioned and in balance with the rest of the dog. The neck is sufficiently long for the nose to reach the ground but is free from throatiness. The topline slopes slightly toward the quarters. The eyes are round and full, dark brown in color. The ears are long and well feathered.

The muzzle is broad with square, even jaws and a scissors bite. The nose is black for most colors, brown for some.

Body and Tail

The chest is deep and wide without interfering with straightforward motion – the ribs are well sprung. The back is strong and evenly sloped from shoulder to tail. The tail is docked and carried in line with the back or slightly higher – it is never carried straight up.

Legs and Feet

The forelegs are straight and strongly boned, the feet compact and large with horny pads. The hindquarters are wide and well-muscled, parallel when in motion and at rest. The hocks are strong and well let down.

Coat and Texture

The coat is short and fine on the head, medium-length on the body with sufficient undercoating. The legs, abdomen, chest, and ears are well feathered but not excessively. The coat is silky and flat or slightly wavy. Trimming should be limited to enhancing the dog's true lines.

Color

Black – Solid black in color – may include tan points and some white on the chest or throat is permissible.

ASCOB – Any solid color other than black; ranges from light cream to dark red, including brown and brown with tan points. Color should be uniform but lighter shade on the feathering is allowed. Some white on the chest or throat is permissible.

Parti-Color – Two or more solid, well-broken colors – one must be white. Permissible combinations include black and white, red and white, brown and white, and roan. Tan markings should be in the same pattern as ASCOB.

Tan Points – Restricted to 10% of the color. Locations may include spot over each eye, sides of the cheeks and muzzle, underside of the ears, feet and legs, under the tail, and on the chest (optional).

Size

The ideal height is 15 inches for adult males and 14 inches for adult females, though height may vary within ½ inch. The length of the body should be sufficient to ensure a straight, free stride.

Gait

The breed shows a typical sporting gait with balanced movement – the gait should be smooth and effortless.

Disqualifications

- Males over 15 ½ inches, females over 14 ½ inches
- Color or combination of colors outside the acceptable standard
- White markings except on the throat and chest in solid color varieties
- Primary color 90% or more in parti-colored varieties
- Tan points in excess of 10%
- Absence of tan markings in Black or ASCOB varieties

English Cocker Spaniel Breed Standard

The AKC accepts both the American Cocker Spaniel and the English Cocker Spaniel for show but these two breeds have separate breed standards. <u>Below you will find an overview of the breed standard for the English Cocker Spaniel breed:</u>

General Appearance and Temperament

The English Cocker Spaniel is an active sporting dog with a compact build. He has a lively temperament and great enthusiasm in the field with a willingness to work. Overall, he is a dog of great balance and no exaggeration of any part.

Head and Neck

The head is strong but free from coarseness, softly contoured. The expression is soft yet alert and intelligent, the eyes medium-sized and dark in color. The ears are set low and well covered in hair, the muzzle equal in length to the skull. The jaws are strong and capable of carrying game with a scissors bite. The nose is black except in livers and brown parti-colors.

Body and Tail

The body is compact, well-knit, and strong with a deep chest but not so wide as to interfere with movement. The ribs are well sprung, the back short and strong. The tail is docked and set to conform to croup – it should be carried horizontally and in constant motion while the dog moves.

Legs and Feet

The shoulders are sloping, the forelegs straight and uniform in size from elbow to heel. The feet are proportionate in size with arched toes and thick pads. The hindquarters are well balanced, the hips broad and the thighs well-muscled.

Coat and Color

The coat is short and fine on the head and medium-length on the body. The hair is silky in texture and flat or slightly wavy, but not curly. The coat should be well-feathered but not so profusely that it will interfere with field work. Trimming is only permitted to enhance the dog's true lines.

Various colors are permissible including solid and parti-color varieties. Parti-colors should be clearly marked, ticked, or roaned with solid markings broken on the body and distributed more or less evenly. Solid colors are black, liver, or red with some white on the chest or throat acceptable.

Size

Adult males should be 16 to 17 inches at the withers, adult females 15 to 16 inches – deviations in size will be penalized. Ideal weights are 28 to 34 pounds for adult males, 26 to 32 pounds for adult females.

Gait

The English Cocker Spaniel has a powerful, frictionless gait and he is capable of covering ground effortlessly, penetrating dense cover to flush out and retrieve game. He moves in a straight line, carrying his head proudly.

Preparing Your Cocker Spaniel for Show

Once you've determined that your Cocker Spaniel is a good representation of the official breed standard, then you can think about entering him in a dog show. Dog shows occur all year-round in many different locations so check the AKC or Kennel Club website for shows in your area.

Remember, the rules for each show will be different so make sure to do your research so that you and your Cocker Spaniel are properly prepared for the show.

On the following page you will find a list of some general and specific recommendations to follow during show prep:

- Ensure that you've chosen the right show for your Cocker Spaniel – the AKC only accepts both the American Cocker Spaniel and the English Cocker Spaniel but they are classified as separate breeds.

- Make sure that your Cocker Spaniel is properly socialized to be in an environment with many other dogs and people.

- Ensure that your Cocker Spaniel is completely housetrained and able to hold his bladder for at least several hours.

- Solidify your dog's grasp of basic obedience – he should listen and follow basic commands.

- Do some research to learn the requirements for specific shows before you choose one – make sure your dog meets all the requirements for registration.

- Make sure that your Cocker Spaniel is caught up on his vaccinations (especially Bordetella since he will be around other dogs) and have your vet clear his overall health for show.

- Have your dog groomed about a week before the show and then take the necessary steps to keep his coat clean and in good condition.

In addition to making sure that your Cocker Spaniel meets the requirements for the show and is a good representation of the AKC breed standard, you should also pack a bag of supplies that you will need on the day of show. <u>Below you will find a list of helpful things to include in your dog show supply pack</u>:

- Registration information
- Dog crate or exercise pen
- Grooming table and grooming supplies
- Food and treats
- Food and water bowls
- Trash bags
- Medication (if needed)
- Change of clothes
- Food/water for self
- Paper towels or rags

- Toys for the dog

If you want to show your Cocker Spaniel but you don't want to jump immediately into an AKC show, you may be able to find some local dog shows in your area. Local shows may be put on by a branch of a national Cocker Spaniel breed club and they can be a great place to learn and to connect with other Cocker Spaniel owners.

Chapter Ten: Keeping Your Dog Healthy

As a dog owner, it is your job to make sure that your Cocker Spaniel gets everything he needs to stay healthy. Giving your dog a healthy diet is one of the primary factors in determining his long-term health and wellbeing, but you also need to make sure he sees the vet on a regular basis. In addition to routine vet check-ups you need to keep an eye on your dog's behavior and condition – the more you know about your dog, the sooner you will be able to catch the early signs and symptoms of disease. In this chapter you will learn about conditions commonly affecting the Cocker Spaniel and about recommended vaccinations.

Common Health Problems Affecting Cocker Spaniels

For the most part, the Cocker Spaniel is a fairly healthy breed but, like all dogs, is prone to certain health problems. According to a Kennel Club survey, the number-one cause of death for Cocker Spaniels is cancer, followed by old age. These dogs are also prone to certain inherited conditions and communicable diseases as well as breed-specific health problems. In this section you will receive an overview of some of the conditions most commonly affecting the Cocker Spaniel breed.

Some of the common conditions affecting Cocker Spaniels include:

- Allergies
- Autoimmune Hemolytic Anemia
- Cherry Eye
- Congenital Deafness
- Epilepsy
- Eye Problems
- Hip Dysplasia
- Hypothyroidism
- Otitis Externa
- Patellar Luxation

Allergies

Just like humans, dogs can develop allergic reactions to a number of different things including medications, certain foods, dust, and other environmental pollutants. An allergy develops when the dog's immune system identifies a substance as pathogenic, or dangerous, and it launches an attack. Allergens can be inhaled, ingested, or taken into the body through skin contact. Dogs can develop allergies at any time and some breeds are more prone to allergies than others such as Cocker Spaniels, Terriers, Retrievers, Setters, and brachycephalic breeds like Pugs and Bulldogs.

Common symptoms of allergies in dogs including red or itchy skin, runny eyes, increased scratching, ear infections, sneezing, vomiting, diarrhea, and swollen paws. Some common allergens for dogs include smoke, pollen, mold, dust, dander, feathers, fleas, medications, cleaning products, certain fabrics, and certain foods. Surprisingly, food allergies tend to produce skin-related symptoms like itching and scratching rather than digestive symptoms. Chronic ear infections are also a common sign of food allergies in dogs. The best treatment for allergies is avoiding contact with the allergen. For some environmental allergens, your vet might prescribe antihistamines or your vet might give your dog an injection to protect him.

Autoimmune Hemolytic Anemia

Sometimes shortened to AIHA, autoimmune hemolytic anemia is a condition in which the dog's immune system starts to destroy its own blood cells. Anemia is a term used to refer to reduced blood cell count. Autoimmune hemolytic anemia is reduced blood cell count resulting from autoimmune activity. In dogs suffering from AIHA, the bone marrow continues to produce red blood cells normally, but once the cells are released into the blood stream they have a reduced lifespan.

There are two types of AIHA – primary and secondary. Primary, or idiopathic AIHA, occurs when the immune system fails to work properly and produces antibodies that target the body's own red blood cells. In secondary AIHA, the surface of existing blood cells becomes altered by some toxin or internal bodily process which leads the immune system to identify them as foreign invaders. In both cases, the cells are destroyed once the immune system identifies them as a target.

Common symptoms of AIHA include pale gums, listlessness, reduced exercise tolerance, and disorientation resulting from low oxygen levels in the blood. Severe cases may be treated with blood transfusions while secondary AIHA is usually treated according to the underlying cause of the problem. Relapses are common with this disease.

Cherry Eye

Although it is not a painful condition, cherry eye can impact your dog's ability to see properly. This condition is the result of a prolapsed gland in the eyelid and it takes the form of a pink mass protruding from the lid. This mass can develop in one or both eyes and it is generally caused by a hereditary weakness of the tissue attaching the gland to the eye. This condition can occur in any breed but it seems to be more common in Cocker Spaniels, Beagles, Bulldogs, Shih Tzus, and Bloodhounds.

Because cherry eye is not a painful or dangerous condition, your veterinarian may opt not to treat it aggressively. In cases where the prolapse becomes enlarged or if it starts to affect your dog's vision, the vet might elect to surgically remove the gland or to simply put it back in place. In some cases, the condition can be treated with topical anti-inflammatories to reduce swelling. Once the condition has been treated you should keep an eye on your dog to keep condition from recurring.

Congenital Deafness

One condition that has been known to affect Cocker Spaniels but is still fairly rare is congenital deafness. This condition is most commonly seen in English Cocker Spaniels that carry white or piebald color genes – this kind of hereditary deafness is also associated to some degree with blue eye color. In dogs that carry these genes, the blood supply to the inner ear degenerates sometime around the three- to four-week mark. The result is complete deafness in one or both ears and it is permanent.

It is fairly easy to diagnose deafness in dogs – a veterinarian can usually spot the condition as soon as he walks into the exam room. Some Cocker Spaniels are born deaf and they never experience the sensation of hearing while others develop the condition gradually. In dogs that have normal hearing, puppies usually begin to respond to sound around the 10-day mark. For puppies that are born deaf, you may start to notice subtle signs that something is off, but it could take a few weeks to be sure that the puppy is completely deaf.

Puppies that are deaf sometimes exhibit increased aggression with littermates because they cannot respond to oral cues such as whimpers or yelps of pain. These dogs don't respond to squeaky toys and they do not startle at loud noises. In general, these puppies also tend to display a decreased activity level when compared to normal puppies.

Unfortunately, there is no treatment option available for congenital deafness – it is the job of the dog owner to adapt to the loss of hearing. You may need to keep your dog in the house or confined to a leash because he may not be aware of dangers like moving cars. You might need to train your dog to respond to hand signals instead of verbal cues and the training process may take a little longer. Though there are additional challenges involved, deaf dogs can lead very long and happy lives with the right modifications.

Epilepsy

Epilepsy is a seizure disorder that may manifest in several different ways. In most cases, seizures are preceded by a focal onset phase during which the dog may appear dazed or frightened. During the seizure, the dog typically falls to its side and becomes stiff, salivating profusely and paddling with all four limbs. Canine seizures generally last for 30 to 90 seconds and they most commonly occur while the dog is resting or asleep.

There are two types of canine epilepsy – primary and secondary. Primary epilepsy is also called true epilepsy or idiopathic epilepsy – this type of epilepsy involves seizure with an unknown cause. This condition usually presents between 6 months and 5 years of age and it may have a genetic link. Secondary epilepsy is a condition in which the cause of the seizures can be determined. The most common causes for secondary epilepsy include degenerative disease, developmental problems, toxins/poisoning, infections, metabolic disorders, nutritional deficiencies, and trauma.

Veterinarians use information about the age of onset and pattern of the seizures to make a diagnosis. Treatment options for canine epilepsy may involve anticonvulsant medications and routine monitoring of the dog's health and weight.

Eye Problems

Cocker Spaniels are prone to a number of eye problems, including congenital conditions like cataracts and progressive retinal atrophy. Another common eye problem seen in these dogs is glaucoma. Glaucoma is a very common condition in which the fluid inside the dog's eye builds and creates intraocular pressure that is too high. When the pressure inside the eye increases, it can lead to damage of the internal structures within the eye. If this condition is not treated promptly, it can lead to permanent loss of vision or total blindness for the dog.

There are two types of glaucoma – primary and secondary. Primary glaucoma involves physical or physiological traits that increase the dog's risk for glaucoma – this is usually determined by genetics. Secondary glaucoma occurs when the glaucoma is caused by another condition such as a penetrating wound to the eye or other causes for inflammation. Glaucoma can sometimes be difficult to diagnose in the early stages, but common signs include dilated pupil, cloudiness of the eye, and rubbing the eye. Treatment options include topical solutions to reduce pressure, increase drainage, and to provide pain relief.

Progressive retinal atrophy affects the retina of the eye, the part that receives light and converts it into electrical nerve signals that the brain interprets as vision. Dogs with PRA typically experience arrested retinal development (called retina dysplasia) or early degeneration of the photoreceptors in the eye. Dogs with retinal dysplasia usually develop symptoms within 2 months and are often blind by 1 year.

The signs of PRA vary according to the rate of progression. This disease is not painful and it doesn't affect the outward appearance of the eye. In most cases, dog owners notice a change in the dog's willingness to go down stairs, or to go down a dark hallway – PRA causes night blindness which can progress to total blindness. Unfortunately, there is no treatment or cure for progressive retinal atrophy and no way to slow the progression of the disease. Most dogs with PRA eventually become blind. Fortunately, dogs often adapt well to blindness as long as their environment remains stable.

Cataracts are characterized by an opacity in the lens of the eye which can obstruct the dog's vision. These opacities can be the result of disease, trauma, or old age and they can sometimes be inherited. For the most part, cataracts are not painful but they can sometimes luxate, or slip away from the tissue holding them in place and float around the eye. Sometimes they settle and block fluid drainage which can lead to glaucoma. Cataracts can't be prevented but vision loss can sometimes be corrected with surgery.

Hip Dysplasia

Hip dysplasia is a very common musculoskeletal problem among dogs. In a normal hip, the head of the femur (thigh bone) sits snugly within the groove of the hip joint and it rotates freely within the grove as the dog moves. Hip dysplasia occurs when the femoral head becomes separated from the hip joint – this is called subluxation. This could occur as a result of abnormal joint structure or laxity in the muscles and ligaments supporting the joint.

This condition can present in puppies as young as 5 months of age or in older dogs. The most common symptoms of hip dysplasia include pain or discomfort, limping, hopping, or unwillingness to move. As the condition progresses, the dog's pain will increase and he may develop osteoarthritis. The dog may begin to lose muscle tone and might even become completely lame in the affected joint.

Genetics are the largest risk factor for hip dysplasia, though nutrition and exercise are factors as well. Diagnosis for hip dysplasia is made through a combination of clinical signs, physical exam, and x-rays. Surgical treatments for hip dysplasia are very common and generally highly effective. Medical treatments may also be helpful to reduce osteoarthritis and to manage pain.

Hypothyroidism

This condition is very common in dogs and it can produce a wide variety of symptoms. Hypothyroidism occurs when the thyroid gland fails to produce enough thyroid hormone – this often leads to weigh loss as well as hair and skin problems. Fortunately, this condition is easy to diagnose with a blood test that checks the dog's levels of certain thyroid hormones like T4.

The thyroid is a gland located in your dog's neck close to the voice box, or larynx. The activity of the thyroid is regulated by the pituitary gland in the brain which produces thyroid stimulating hormone (TSH). Hypothyroidism occurs when the thyroid produces insufficient thyroid hormone – this is most often caused by a destruction of the thyroid gland. This is often associated with other diseases like cancer or atrophy of the thyroid tissue. The use of certain medications can affect the thyroid gland as well.

Hypothyroidism is most commonly diagnosed in dogs between 4 and 10 years of age. The main symptoms of this disease include lethargy, hair loss, weight gain, excessive shedding, hyperpigmentation of skin, slow heartrate, high blood cholesterol and anemia. Treatment usually involves daily treatment with synthetic thyroid hormone.

Otitis Externa

Sometimes known as inflammation of the inner ear, otitis externa is a very common condition in Cocker Spaniels. This condition occurs when something happens to change the environment inside the ear canal and the glands inside the ear become enlarged and start to produce excessive amounts of wax. Additionally, the skin inside and outside the ear also begins to produce extra tissue which can cause the ear canal to become inflamed and to narrow.

In many cases, otitis externa is secondary to an underlying condition such as an ear infection. This condition can result in pain, itching, and redness and it can sometimes lead to a ruptured ear drum if the condition becomes chronic. Signs that your dog has this condition may include head shaking, odor coming from the ear, and scratching at the external flaps of the ear. Upon physical examination you will also see that the tissues are red and swollen.

Otitis externa can be caused by a variety of things including parasites, reactions to foreign bodies in the ear, reactions to drugs, food allergies, buildup of dead skin cells, or even autoimmune disease. This condition can usually be treated on an outpatient basis with topical therapy and a complete cleaning of the external ear. Topical therapies may include corticosteroids, antibacterial ointments, or antiseptic drops. Lack of treatment can lead to deafness.

Patellar Luxation

Patellar luxation is a musculoskeletal condition in which the patella (or kneecap) slides out of its normal anatomic position within the groove of the femur (thigh bone). This condition is one of the most common joint abnormalities in dogs and it is particularly common in small and toy breeds like the Cocker Spaniel, Pomeranian, Yorkshire Terrier and the Boston Terrier. It is also more common in female dogs than in male dogs.

In the early stages of the condition, many dogs do not display serious symptoms. They might experience some soreness or tenderness after the patella pops back into place but they may still be able to walk normally. The more frequently the dislocation occurs, however, the more wear and tear on the bone and joint the dog will suffer. This leads to osteoarthritis and pain, potentially even lameness in the joint. The dog generally doesn't experience pain while the kneecap is dislocated, but he will when it pops back into its rightful place.

The cause of patellar luxation is usually the result of a genetic malformation or some kind of trauma. Unfortunately, medical treatments are rarely effective and surgery is usually required to achieve long-term relief. After surgery the dog will need to limit its mobility and regular vet check-ups are recommended.

Preventing Illness with Vaccinations

The best way to keep your Cocker Spaniel healthy is to provide him with a nutritious and balanced diet. You also need to ensure that he gets proper veterinary care, and that includes routine vaccinations. Vaccinations will not protect your Cocker Spaniel against nutritional deficiencies or inherited conditions, but they can help to protect him from certain communicable diseases like rabies, distemper, and parvovirus.

The vaccinations your Cocker Spaniel needs may vary depending where you live since certain regions have a higher risk for certain diseases. Your vet will know which vaccinations your dog needs and when he needs them, but the vaccination schedule below will help you to keep track of when your Cocker Spaniel needs to see the vet.

To give you an idea what kind of vaccinations your puppy will need, consult the vaccination schedule below:

Vaccination Schedule for Dogs**			
Vaccine	**Doses**	**Age**	**Booster**
Rabies	1	12 weeks	annual
Distemper	3	6-16 weeks	3 years
Parvovirus	3	6-16 weeks	3 years
Adenovirus	3	6-16 weeks	3 years
Parainfluenza	3	6 weeks, 12-14 weeks	3 years
Bordetella	1	6 weeks	annual
Lyme Disease	2	9, 13-14 weeks	annual
Leptospirosis	2	12 and 16 weeks	annual
Canine Influenza	2	6-8, 8-12 weeks	annual

** Keep in mind that vaccine requirements may vary from one region to another. Only your vet will be able to tell you which vaccines are most important for the region where you live.

Cocker Spaniel Care Sheet

In reading this book you have received a wealth of valuable information about the Cocker Spaniel and its care. This information will come in handy as you prepare your home for your new puppy and as you get used to life as a dog owner. As you and your Cocker Spaniel get to know each other you may find that you need to reference certain bits of information from this book. Rather than flipping through the entire book, use this care sheet to reference key facts and tidbits about the Cocker Spaniel breed.

1.) Basic Cocker Spaniel Information

Pedigree: exact origins unknown, developed from field spaniels in Spain

AKC Group: Sporting Group

Breed Size: small to medium

Height: 13.5 to 16 inches (34 - 41 cm), depending on sex/type

Weight: 24 to 32 lbs. (11 to 15 kg)

Coat Length: medium-long; shorter on the head and back

Coat Texture: silky and fine; flat or wavy

Shedding: moderate, frequent grooming needed

Color: many colors and patterns; solid as well as parti-color, often with tan color points

Eyes and Nose: dark; black or brown, depending on type

Ears: drop ears; large, long and well feathered

Tail: docked short, carried horizontally

Temperament: sweet, affectionate, lively, playful, loyal, intelligent, trainable

Strangers: may bark at strangers

Children: generally good with children but should be supervised around young children

Other Dogs: generally good with other dogs if properly trained and socialized

Training: intelligent and very trainable

Exercise Needs: moderately active, does not require a great deal of exercise; 30-minute daily walk recommended

Health Conditions: allergies, autoimmune hemolytic anemia, cherry eye, congenital deafness, epilepsy, eye problems, hip dysplasia, hypothyroidism, otitis externa, and patellar luxation

Lifespan: average 12 to 15 years

2.) Habitat Requirements

Recommended Accessories: crate, dog bed, food/water dishes, toys, collar, leash, harness, grooming supplies

Collar and Harness: sized by weight

Grooming Supplies: wire pin brush, slicker brush, metal wide-tooth comb

Grooming Frequency: brush daily; professional grooming every 6 to 8 weeks

Energy Level: moderate, not overly active

Exercise Requirements: 30 minute walk daily

Crate: highly recommended

Crate Size: just large enough for dog to lie down and turn around comfortably

Crate Extras: lined with blanket or plush pet bed

Food/Water: stainless steel or ceramic bowls, clean daily

Toys: start with an assortment, see what the dog likes; include some mentally stimulating toys

Exercise Ideas: play games to give your dog extra exercise during the day; train your dog for various dog sports

3.) Nutritional Needs

Nutritional Needs: water, protein, carbohydrate, fats, vitamins, minerals

Calorie Needs: varies by age, weight, and activity level

Amount to Feed (puppy): feed freely but consult recommendations on the package

Amount to Feed (adult): consult recommendations on the package; calculated by weight

Feeding Frequency: two to three meals daily

Important Ingredients: fresh animal protein (chicken, beef, lamb, turkey, eggs), digestible carbohydrates (rice, oats, barley), animal fats

Important Minerals: calcium, phosphorus, potassium, magnesium, iron, copper and manganese

Important Vitamins: Vitamin A, Vitamin A, Vitamin B-12, Vitamin D, Vitamin C

Look For: AAFCO statement of nutritional adequacy; protein at top of ingredients list; no artificial flavors, dyes, preservatives

4.) Breeding Information

Age of First Heat: around 6 months (or earlier)

Heat (Estrus) Cycle: 14 to 21 days

Frequency: twice a year, every 6 to 7 months

Breeding Age: at least 2 years old, no more than 8

Breeding Pair: both good examples of the breed standard; breed solid to solid and parti-color to parti-color

Time Between Litters: at least one heat cycle, ideally one year

Greatest Fertility: 11 to 15 days into the cycle

Gestation Period: 61 to 65 days, average 63 days

Pregnancy Detection: possible after 21 days, best to wait 28 days before exam

Feeding Pregnant Dogs: maintain normal diet until week 5 or 6 then slightly increase rations

Signs of Labor: body temperature drops below normal 100° to 102°F (37.7° to 38.8°C), may be as low as 98°F (36.6°C); dog begins nesting in a dark, quiet place

Contractions: period of 10 minutes in waves of 3 to 5 followed by a period of rest

Whelping: puppies are born in 1/2 hour increments following 10 to 30 minutes of forceful straining

Puppies: born with eyes and ears closed; eyes open at 3 weeks, teeth develop at 10 weeks

Litter Size: 1 to 7 puppies, average 5 or 6

Size at Birth: about 8 to 8.5 ounces (250g)

Weaning: start offering puppy food soaked in water at 6 weeks; fully weaned by 8 weeks

Socialization: start as early as possible to prevent puppies from being nervous as an adult

Index

C

D

E

F

G

H

I

K

L

M

N

O

P

R

S

T

U

V

W

Y

References

"AAFCO Dog Food Nutrient Profiles." DogFoodAdvisor. <http://www.dogfoodadvisor.com/frequently-asked-questions/aafco-nutrient-profiles/>

"American Cocker Spaniel." DogBreedInfo.com. <http://www.dogbreedinfo.com/americancocker.htm>

"American Cocker Spaniel Health Problems." Your Purebred Puppy. <http://www.yourpurebredpuppy.com/health/americancockerspaniels.html>

"Annual Dog Care Costs." PetFinder. <https://www.petfinder.com/pet-adoption/dog-adoption/annual-dog-care-costs/>

"Caloric Requirements for Your Dog." Tails. <http://www.tails.co/requirements.html>

"Canine Dental Disease." Banfield Pet Hospital. <http://www.banfield.com/pet-health-resources/preventive-care/dental/canine-dental-disease>

"Caring for a New Puppy." Cocker Puppies for Sale. <http://cockerpuppiesforsale.weebly.com/cocker-spaniel-puppies-blog/archives/07-2011/3>

"Choosing a Healthy Puppy." WebMD. <http://pets.webmd.com/dogs/guide/choosing-healthy-

"Cocker Spaniel." DogTime.com. <http://dogtime.com/dog-breeds/cocker-spaniel>

"Cocker Spaniel." VetStreet. <http://www.vetstreet.com/dogs/cocker-spaniel>

"Cocker Spaniel Breeding Advice." Cocker Spaniel Stud Dogs. <http://www.cockerspanielstuddogs.co.uk/studding-check-list.asp>

"Cocker Spaniel Grooming." ILoveCockerSpaniels.net. <http://ilovecockerspaniels.net/how-to-groom-a-cocker-spaniel/>

"Cocker Spaniel Grooming Profile." PetGroomer.com. <http://www.petgroomer.com/Grooming101/Breeds/cocker_spaniel.htm>

"How to Be a Responsible Cocker Spaniel Breeder." Zim Family Cockers. <http://www.zimfamilycockers.com/breeding.html>

"How to Find a Responsible Breeder." HumaneSociety.org. <http://www.humanesociety.org/issues/puppy_mills/tips/finding_responsible_dog_breeder.html?referrer=https://www.google.com/>

"Most Popular Dog Breeds in America." AKC.org. <http://www.akc.org/news/the-most-popular-dog-breeds-in-america/>

"My Bowl: What Goes into a Balanced Diet for Your Dog?" PetMD. <http://www.petmd.com/dog/slideshows/nutrition-center/my-bowl-what-goes-into-a-balanced-diet-for-your-dog>

"Nutrients Your Dog Needs." ASPCA.org.
<https://www.aspca.org/pet-care/dog-care/nutrients-your-dog-needs>

"Nutrition: General Feeding Guidelines for Dogs." VCA
Animal Hospitals. <http://www.vcahospitals.com/
main/pet-health-information/article/animal-
health/nutrition-general-feeding-guidelines-for-dogs/6491>

"Official Standard for the American Cocker Spaniel." AKC.
<http://images.akc.org/pdf/breeds/standards/CockerSpanie
l.pdf?_ga=1.16904953.1751144016.1454425532>

"Official Standard for the English Cocker Spaniel." AKC.
<http://images.akc.org/pdf/breeds/standards/EnglishCocke
rSpaniel.pdf?_ga=1.251215302.1751144016.1454425532>

"Pet Care Costs." ASPCA.org. <https://www.aspca.org/
adopt/pet-care-costs>

"Puppy Proofing Your Home." Hill's Pet.
<http://www.hillspet.com/dog-care/puppy-proofing-your-
home.html>

"Puppy Proofing Your Home." PetEducation.com.
<http://www.peteducation.com/article.cfm?c=2+2106&aid=
3283>

"Tips on Whelping a Litter of Puppies." Zim Family
Cockers. <http://www.zimfamilycockers.com/
whelping.html>

Vitamins and Minerals Your Dog Needs." Kim Boatman. The Dog Daily. <http://www.thedogdaily.com/dish/diet/ dogs_vitamins/index.html#.VHOtMPnF_IA>

"What's the Ideal Cocker Spaniel Diet?" About Cocker Spaniels. <http://www.about-cocker-spaniels.com/cocker-spaniel-diet.html>

Photo Credits

**All photos purchased from BigStockPhoto.net unless otherwise noted below:

Page X (English Cocker Spaniel) by Gergely Vass via Wikimedia Commons, < ttps://en.wikipedia.org/wiki/ Cocker_Spaniel#/media/File:EnglishCockerSpaniel_simon.jp g>

Page X (American Cocker Spaniel) by Tomacnha via Wikimedia Commons, <https://en.wikipedia.org/wiki/ Cocker_Spaniel#/media/File:American_Cocker_in_Tallinn_5. JPG>

Feeding Baby
Cynthia Cherry
978-1941070000

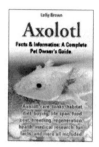

Axolotl
Lolly Brown
978-0989658430

Dysautonomia, POTS
Syndrome
Frederick Earlstein
978-0989658485

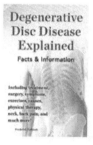

Degenerative Disc
Disease Explained
Frederick Earlstein
978-0989658485

Sinusitis, Hay Fever,
Allergic Rhinitis Explained
Frederick Earlstein
978-1941070024

Wicca
Riley Star
978-1941070130

Zombie Apocalypse
Rex Cutty
978-1941070154

Capybara
Lolly Brown
978-1941070062

Eels As Pets
Lolly Brown
978-1941070167

Scabies and Lice Explained
Frederick Earlstein
978-1941070017

Saltwater Fish As Pets
Lolly Brown
978-0989658461

Torticollis Explained
Frederick Earlstein
978-1941070055

Kennel Cough
Lolly Brown
978-0989658409

Physiotherapist, Physical
Therapist
Christopher Wright
978-0989658492

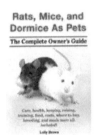

Rats, Mice, and Dormice
As Pets
Lolly Brown
978-1941070079

Wallaby and Wallaroo Care
Lolly Brown
978-1941070031

Bodybuilding Supplements
Explained
Jon Shelton
978-1941070239

Demonology
Riley Star
978-19401070314

Pigeon Racing
Lolly Brown
978-1941070307

Dwarf Hamster
Lolly Brown
978-1941070390

Cryptozoology
Rex Cutty
978-1941070406

Eye Strain
Frederick Earlstein
978-1941070369

Inez The Miniature Elephant
Asher Ray
978-1941070353

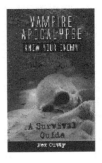

Vampire Apocalypse
Rex Cutty
978-1941070321

Made in the USA
Coppell, TX
20 February 2022